First published in 1999 by
Mercier Press
PO Box 5 5 French Church St Cork
Tel: (021) 275040; Fax: (021) 274969; e.mail: books@mercier.ie
16 Hume Street Dublin 2
Tel: (01) 661 5299; Fax: (01) 661 8583; e.mail: books@marino.ie

Trade enquiries to CMD Distribution 55A Spruce Avenue
Stillorgan Industrial Park Blackrock County Dublin
Tel: (01) 294 2556; Fax: (01) 294 2564
e.mail: cmd@columba.ie

© Peg Coghlan 1999
A CIP record for this book is available from the British Library.

ISBN 1 85635 213 7
10 9 8 7 6 5 4 3 2 1

Cover photograph courtesy of Bord Fáilte
Cover design by Penhouse Design

THE BLARNEY STONE

THE BLARNEY STONE

PEG COGHLAN

MERCIER PRESS

There is a stone there,
That whoever kisses,
Oh! he never misses
To grow eloquent.

Francis Sylvester Mahoney

CONTENTS

1   Setting the Scene   9
2   The Blarney Stone
      in Song and Story   14
3   Cormac Láidir, His Castle
      and His Stone   26
4   Romancing the Stone   36
5   The Blarney Stone
      and the Diaspora   46
6   Odes to Blarney   52
     Appendix   73
     Select Bibliography   78

1

SETTING THE SCENE

The village of Blarney lies five miles northwest of the city of Cork on the bank of the Shournagh River. Its distinctive features are its elegant appearance, the refurbished woollen mills and the castle demesne, which lies to the southwest of the village. The position is scenically idyllic and was an appropriate place for the MacCarthys, the local chieftains, to build a strong fortification. The first structure, probably of wood with protective mound and palisade, was erected in the tenth century on an isolated limestone crag. The first stone building was constructed around 1210 and this, enlarged and improved in 1446, is the Blarney Castle which, rising out of its surroundings of immemorial trees, so impresses the crowds of visitors that come year-round to kiss that most famous of stones.

Between 1765 and 1782, the then owner of the Blarney estate, Sir John Jeffreyes, created the village of Blarney and began the manufacture of linen and woollen goods, especially tweeds. At one time, he had thirteen spinning mills in operation. The industry was taken over in 1824 by a local family called Mahony, and the Blarney Woollen Mills continued to turn out quality goods for 150 years. The present-day visitor will discover that the mills have been transformed into an elegant tourist centre with shops, hotel, restaurants and a display of material from the heyday of the industry.

The Blarney estate was acquired by marriage in 1846 by the Colthurst family, who built the fine Scottish-baronial house in the castle demesne (completed in 1874) which is the family home to this day. It is open to visitors for most of the year and since the Colthursts do use it for some months annually it strikes the visitor as a home and not just a house.

Samuel Lewis, who compiled the monumental *Topographical Dictionary of Ireland* in 1837, describes the castle as 'a picturesque ruin', the top of which:

commands a very fine view over a rich undulating tract intersected by the rivers Blarney, Comane and Scorthonac, and bounded on the north-west by the lofty chain of the Boggra mountains. On the east is the Comane bog, many years since an impenetrable wilderness, and the last receptacle for wolves in this part of the country: that river, which takes its name from its serpentine course, flows through the bog and joins the river Blarney under the walls of the castle; and their united waters receive a considerable accession from the Scorthonac, a rapid stream which rises in the Boggra mountains.

The many natural beauties of the place, which include 'spacious natural caves', were improved by importation by the Jeffreyes family of exotic trees and shrubbery so that the 'groves of Blarney', already well known to and appreciated by the citizens of Cork, took on the appearance and often the atmosphere of a pleasure garden. Anna Maria Fielding (1800–81) who, with the help of her husband Samuel

Carter Hall (1800–89), did most to give an honest picture of Ireland to the English in *Ireland, its Scenery, Characters, etc.* (1840) visited the demesne while doing the necessary travels for her book and was naturally more impressed by the 'Italian improvements' the owners had made in the previous century than by the slightly vulgar pursuit of eloquence through the stone.

We visited 'The sweet Rock-close' – it well deserves the epithet – during a sunny day in June; and never can we forget the fragrant shade afforded by the luxuriant evergreens which seem rooted in the limestone rock; the little river Comane is guarded by a natural terrace, fringed by noble trees; several of the spaces between are grottos – natural also; some with seats, where many a love tale has been told, and will be, doubtless, as long as Cork lads and lasses indulge in pic-nic fêtes, while the blackbird whistles, and the wood-pigeon coos in the twisted foliage above their heads ... We wandered from the shades of the Rock-close across the green and richly-wooded pastures that lead to the lake. The scene here is English rather than Irish, but every step is hallowed by a legend: it is implicitly believed that the last Earl of Clancarty who inhabited the castle, committed the keeping of his plate to the deepest waters, and that it will never be recovered until a MacCarthy be again lord of Blarney.

Even today the Rock Close, with its circle of stones and age-old trees, keeps its eighteenth-century air of a pleasure dell.

2

THE BLARNEY STONE
IN SONG AND STORY

The southern city of Cork was a prosperous place in the early years of the nineteenth century and prosperity meant leisure, at least for the burghers and their families, who regarded the journey to Blarney as a pleasant airing and a visit to 'the purling of sweet silent streams' as relief from urban crowds and odours.

The city at the time was in the throes of what has since been defined as 'Second-City Syndrome' affecting such places as Glasgow, Manchester, Chicago, Florence and Melbourne. These cities elevated their 'secondness' to a virtue and strove to prove that they were far from provincial, and what if they were! They had none of the Big Smoke's brashness, insensitivity, unfriendliness and vice. In those days of slow and uncomfortable travel, when it was preferable to go from Dublin to Cork by sea or canal, the Corkonians, as they self-consciously called themselves, had to establish their own urban culture and amenities. Cork was less static and more entrepreneurial than Dublin had become after losing its own parliament by the Act of Union with Great Britain (1801), and there were many opportunities for wild sports and genteel pastimes.

Part of the intellectual life of Cork was centred in the 'Forty-five Club', so named because prospective members were required to join in forty-five consecutive rounds of punch. The leader was William Maginn (1793–1842), a precocious and talented classicist who graduated from Trinity College Dublin at eighteen years of age and returned to Cork to teach in his father's private school. His coterie was sometimes known as 'The Fraserians' because he was one of the founders of *Fraser's Magazine*. Two of his associates, the elderly Richard Alfred Milliken (1767–1815) and the bright young Francis Sylvester Mahony (1804–1866), probably have most responsibility to bear for the whole cult of Blarney and its stone.

The MacCarthys, chieftains of Blarney, had for centuries maintained a bardic school and even after the decline of the Gaelic tradition in the seventeenth and eighteenth centuries, the tradition of 'courts' of poetry persisted in Munster. By the beginning of the nineteenth century the local poets had tried their hands at English. The results of applying Gaelic forms and techniques made, at least at the start, for what the Anglo-Irish of Cork such as the members of the 'Forty-five Club' considered absurdity. One such local piece, 'Castlehyde', was sold in broadsheet, and such innocent lines as: 'The buck, the doe, the fox, the eagle, they skip and play by the river side' caused the Cork wits a deal of merriment. (Castlehyde was a demesne similar to Blarney on the Blackwater near Fermoy, about twenty miles north of Blarney.) After a reading of the poem at a convivial evening in 1798, Milliken accepted the challenge to write a parody of it. The express result was the poem 'The Groves of Blarney'. One verse, as was common in the courtly poetry it was mocking, is a tribute to the chatelaine of the castle:

'Tis Lady Jeffers
That owns this station;
Like Alexander,
Or Queen Helen fair;
There's no commander
In all the nation,
For emulation,
Can with her compare.
Such walls surround her,
That no nine-pounder
Could dare to plunder
Her place of strength;
But Oliver Cromwell,
Her he did pommel
And made a breach
In her battlement.

The poem, which is subscripted, 'Air: Castle-hyde', quickly became popular. The tune of 'Castlehyde' is almost the same as that used by Thomas Moore for 'The Last Rose of Summer', which was itself based on an old Irish air. Milliken's squib passed into the repertory, in spite of such poetical conceits as 'And comely eels in verdant mud'. It suffered the same fate as Swift's *Gulliver's Travels* and Mahony's lampoon 'The Bells of Shandon', which was intended as a parody of a Moore's 'Melody'. Both were taken seriously, the first as a straightforward fantasy-adventure story for children, the second as a sentimental Cork anthem, in spite of such rhymes as 'grand on/Shandon' and 'Moscow/kiosk o!'

It is clear that when Milliken picked on beautiful Blarney as the subject of his parody of 'Castlehyde' he was either unaware of the tradition of the magical stone or, more probably, did not think it worthy of mention.

Unlike Milliken, who was a native of Castlemartyr, a village twenty miles east of Cork on the road to Youghal, his young friend and co-Fraserian, Francis Sylvester Mahony, was actually born in Blarney, a son of the woollen manufacturer. Mahony claimed the right, some time in the 1820s, about ten years after the original author's death, to add to Milliken's effusion. Like his companions he had literary leanings, although his work, written under the pseudonym of 'Father Prout', became much better known than theirs. He had begun to train as a Jesuit, left Clongowes in disgrace but was ordained a priest at Lucca in Tuscany in 1832. Mahony ministered for two years in a Cork parish before leaving after a row with his bishop. He was of all the members of the group the one most acquainted with Blarney and its traditions, and it is in his additional verse that the magical qualities of the Blarney stone get their first literary mention.

There is a boat on
The lake to float on.
And lots of beauties
Which I can't entwine;
But were I a preacher,
Or a classics teacher
In every feature
I'd make them shine!
There is a stone there.
That whoever kisses,
Oh! he never misses
To grow eloquent;
'Tis he may clamber
To a lady's chamber,
Or become a member

Of parliament.
A clever spouter
He'll soon turn out, or
An out-and-outer,
To be let alone.
Don't hope to hinder him,
Or to bewilder him,
Sure he's a pilgrim
From the Blarney stone!

The in-jokes about 'preacher' and 'classics teacher' aside, this is a comment about an existing
tradition. Although Mahony's was the first
mention in verse of the marvellous capacity of
the Blarney stone to give eloquent speech to
'those who might salute it', there must have
already existed a tradition about the magical
properties of the stone and the place. Even
before the turn of the nineteenth century, visitors
were directed towards the castle tower and the
stone that was set in its wall. The rapidly
growing interest in the stone coincided with the
realisation by British visitors after the Act of
Union in 1801 that Ireland, although never
quite quiescent politically, was a fascinating

place to visit. Its beauties, though pleasing to the 'romantic' eye, were not as stern and wild as those of Sir Walter Scott's 'Caledonia', and once the sea voyage was accomplished, travel was not so difficult as in the Highlands.

Mahony was noted for his sense of mischief and he may have given the stone more credit than it was entitled to, but he wrote about what was already part of local and tourist lore. Certainly by 1840, when Lewis was compiling his *Topographical Dictionary*, the tradition was well established:

The interest which both natives and strangers take in the castle arises more from a tradition connected with a stone in its north-eastern angle, about 20 feet from the top, than from any other circumstances: this stone, which bears an inscription in Latin recording the erection of the fortress, is called the 'Blarney stone,' and has given rise to the well known phrase of 'Blarney,' in reference to a notion that, if any one kisses it, he will ever after have a cajoling tongue and the art of flattery or of telling lies with unblushing effrontery.

By 1825, ten years after the death of Milliken, who had first put the name of Blarney into English poetry, the cult of the stone was such that distinguished visitors could not escape it. When Sir Walter Scott himself came to Munster in 1825, he made the necessary visit to the lakes of Killarney, Blarney's nearest rival. Then in the company of his son-in-law (and biographer) John Gibson Lockhart (1794–1854) and 'the noted Irish authoress', Maria Edgeworth (1767–1849), he had 'a right mirthful picnic' at the castle.

Sir Walter climbed up to the top of the castle, and kissed, with due faith and devotion, the famous Blarney Stone, one salute of which is said to emancipate the pilgrim from all future visitations of *mauvaise honte*.

Mahony, describing this visit in an essay, 'Plea for Pilgrimages', published in *The Reliques of*

Father Prout (1837), gives a prose version of his verses about the stone:

> . . . it is endowed with the property of communicating to the happy tongue that comes in contact with its polished surface the gift of gentle insinuating, with soft talk in all its ramifications, whether employed in vows and promises light in air, such as lead captive the female heart, or elaborate mystification of a grosser grain, such as may do for the House of Commons – all summed up and characterized by the mysterious term *Blarney*.

It is entirely typical of the writings of the period that the person presumed to kiss the stone is invariably a 'he' and that one of the gifts with which 'he' is endowed by the act is the ability to succeed with the 'female heart'. Yet the practice was not confined to men. In the growing business of tourism (the Oxford English Dictionary records the word as early as 1811) women were more than taking their part. *A Little Tour of Ireland* (1859) had illustrations by the *Punch* caricaturist John Leech (1817–64) showing crinolined young women tripping eloquently down the steps of the tower, having kissed the stone.

This gift of eloquence was seen at the time and later as slightly tainted. Writing in defence in the *Cork Historical and Archaeological Journal* (Vol 18, 1912) J. S. Coyne notes:

A popular tradition attributes to the Blarney Stone the power of endowing whoever kisses it with sweet persuasive wheedling eloquence, so perceptible in the language of the Cork people, and which is generally termed Blarney. This is the true meaning of the word and not as some writers have supposed, a faculty of deviating from veracity with an unblushing countenance whenever it may be convenient.

Anna Hall, who wrote a play called *The Groves of Blarney* (1838), failed to see the humour in Milliken's relatively harmless pastiche. She probably forgot that it was a parody of 'Castlehyde' and

There'is a Stone there that whoever kisses   A clever spouter he'll sure turn out or
Oh he never misses to grow eloquint   An out-and-outer to be let alone
Tis he may clamber to a lady's chamber   Dont hope to hinder him, or to bewilder him
Or become a member of Parliament   Shure he's
A PILGRIM at the BLARNEY STONE.

Kissing the original Blarney Stone

GOIN' TO KISS THE RA'AL 'BLARNEY STONE.

With quare sinsashuns and palpitashuns,
A kiss I'll venture here, Mavrone,
'Tis swater Blarney, good Father Mahony,
Kissin' the Girls than that dirty stone.

Practising the 'gift of the gab'

Winston Churchill at the Blarney Stone in 1912
(Examiner Publications)

View from the top of the castle

19th-century pilgrims kissing the Blarney Stone

A more recent pilgrim (Bord Fáilte)

took great exception to the poem:

> It has raised many a laugh at Ireland's
> expense, and contributed largely to aid
> the artist and the actor, of gone-by times,
> in exhibiting the Irishman as little better
> than a buffoon – very amusing, no doubt,
> but exciting any feeling rather than that
> of respect.

Like many exiles, she was over-protective of her countrypeople, especially as she considered herself their moral ambassador in Britain. She tended to urge on them admonitions to self-improvement and was perhaps, as William Carleton suggested, not quite in sympathy with them.

3

CORMAC LÁIDIR, HIS CASTLE AND HIS STONE

When the substantial castle of Blarney was built by Cormac MacCarthy (1411–94) in 1446, the fatal connection with England was no threat to the power of individual Irish lords. MacCarthy may have been called Fourth Lord of Muskerry by Henry VI of England, to whom he owed a kind of fealty, but he was undisputed chief in his territory. His castle had walls eighteen feet thick and the surviving tower that holds the famous stone rose to over 120 feet. Time and delapidation have, however, reduced the keep's height to eighty-five feet. Cormac MacCarthy's sobriquet *láidir* (strong) was applicable both physically and politically, and his castle was known as the strongest fortress in all Munster. Into its tower wall he had a stone inserted with the inscription: *Cormac MacCarthy Fortis Me Fieri Fecit AD 1446* ('Cormac MacCarthy the Strong caused me to be built in the year of Our Lord 1446'). The frivolous visitor who called himself 'An Oxonian' when he wrote *A Little Tour of Ireland* in 1859 translated this as:

> Cormac Macarthy, bould as bricks,
> Made me in Fourteen Forty-six.

The tower is the last relic of the cluster of buildings that once stood on the site, forming what was essentially a fortified town, inside the walls of which the local peasantry would find shelter in time of attack. Danger could come from rival chieftains establishing property rights or avenging insults – the usual pattern of Irish life in the Middle Ages. More serious was the threat of conquest by the English, all the more likely under the Protestant Tudors, whose attitude to the native Irish aristocracy had two elements: fear of the counter-reformation forces of Catholic Europe and the need for ever greater amounts of plunder.

The MacCarthys hadn't held power in Blarney

for 500 years without learning something of the brass tacks of politics. Succeeding chieftains took the side that promised advantage. When Hugh O'Neill risked all at the Battle of Kinsale in 1601 the MacCarthys supported the English. Cormac McDermod MacCarthy, on orders from Sir George Carew, Elizabeth I's President of Munster, marched a thousand Muskerry soldiers to the Spanish lines to demonstrate that the local Irish supported the queen.

Relations between the MacCarthys and the Virgin Queen had been curious. Elizabeth I very much wanted to avoid trouble in Ireland, sensing that the country was destined to be a persistent thorn in England's side. She would have been content with minimum loyalty and maximum tribute, and she put a lot of effort into securing O'Neill with the hope that as Earl of Tyrone he would acquiesce in her plan for Ireland.

That hope ended with the Battle of Kinsale but Elizabeth expected that MacCarthy would graciously submit to the orders of Carew and replace old practices with those approved by the English. The Lord of Blarney believed that he had done enough by marching his men to Kinsale. He did not feel much like having a garrison of English soldiers in his precious castle and he had no relish of the English system of tenure which was part of the deal. Daily Carew's officers presented themselves but were met by long, eloquent, cajoling speeches, promising much but delivering little. As Crofton Croker the Munster antiquary (1798–1854) put it in *Researches in the South of Ireland* (1824), '[Cormac] kept protocolising with soft promises and delusive delays.' When the state of things was communicated to the queen she is supposed to have said: 'This is all Blarney; what he says he never means.' (The word passed into the language and was defined by the OED as 'the art of flattery or of telling lies with unblushing effrontery' and given a literary citing as early as 1819. It was usually a noun but it could also be a verb.)

The blarneying proved effective, for the MacCarthys held on to their castle. Cormac Dermod was succeeded by Cormac Óg, who accepted the English offer of what Henry VIII had called 'surrender and regrant', and was created Lord Viscount Muskerry and Baron of Blarney by Charles I. His eldest son Donagh succeeded in 1640, and held so much land and emoluments that he was one of the richest subjects of the king. The following year the rising of the Ulstermen, who had been dispossessed by the plantations, against the Scots and English 'undertakers' plunged the country into turmoil again. To add to the confusion, Charles I was about to engage in civil war with the forces of Parliament. The MacCarthys were Catholic and strongly royalist, and Lord Muskerry, as Donagh MacCarthy was called, was one of the members of the Supreme Council of the Confederation of Kilkenny. The story of the Eleven Years War (1641–52) is very complicated but it is certain that the Cromwellian leader, Roger Boyle, Baron Broghill, took Blarney Castle with little resistance in 1646, the Lord of Blarney being away supporting the king, as a personal friend of his eldest son Charles.

It was no surprise that Cromwell's success in annihilating the Royalist-Catholic forces of the Confederation should have led to the confiscation of MacCarthy lands. In 1652 Broghill was confirmed in his acquisitions, 'in satisfaction for the eminent services he has performed for the Commonwealth, and are to be enjoyed by him, his heirs, etc. by virtue of the Acts of Parliament passed for this purpose'. The rightful owner of Blarney was by this time in Europe, attending upon his royal master.

Broghill was allowed to keep the Blarney estate for just eight years; the seventeenth was a see-saw century as far as the fortunes of the Irish aristocracy were concerned. When Charles II returned as king in 1660, Viscount Muskerry was further honoured as the Earl of Clancarty, and since his wife was the sister of James Butler, Duke of Ormond, Lord Lieutenant of Ireland, his lands were immediately restored to him. Broghill, though pardoned like most of the king's enemies, had to return to his original home in Cork.

By blarney and other means Clancarty became one of the greatest landowners in Ireland and remained a strong supporter of the often ungrateful Stuarts until his death. His grandson, also Donagh, was one of the first to welcome James II when he landed at Kinsale in 1688 in his attempt to win back the English crown from William of Orange. He led a regiment of Muskerry men to join the Jacobite forces in a vain attempt to raise the Siege of Derry in 1689 and was taken prisoner in the battle for Cork in 1690 by the first Churchill, the Duke of Marlborough. He escaped from the Tower of London to France, where he was joined by other Wild Geese, and two years later the castle and groves of Blarney were auctioned in Dublin.

They were bought by Sir Richard Pine, Lord Chief Justice of Ireland, who then resold the estate to Sir James Jeffreyes. James II died in 1701 and two attempts, in 1715 and 1745, failed to set up his son James (1688–1768, 'the king over the water' of the Jacobite toast) as James III. Jeffreyes was confirmed in his lands and the long rule of the MacCarthys was over. The Jeffreyes family (the spelling of the name varies) were on the whole benevolent and responsible landlords who did their best for their Irish tenants. The elegant appearance of Blarney, with its village green and the 'groves' which show evidence of fashionable Georgian landscaping, and the reputation of the demesne as an amenity for the Cork citizens are due in large measure to this enterprising family. Arthur Young (1741–1820), the agriculturalist, whose book *A Tour in Ireland* (1778) gives so much information about Irish rural life in the eighteenth century, visited the village and found it an example of what a small town should be.

> The town is built in a square, composed of a large handsome inn, and manu-facturers' houses, all built of excellent stone, limestone and slate. A church by the first fruits and liberal addition of £300 from Mr Jeffreys. A market house in which are sold a hundred pounds worth of knit stockings per week. Four bridges which he obtained from the county, and another (the flat arch) to which he contributed a considerable sum.

Young goes on to list the various industries that the Jeffreyes of the time had begun: mills for bleaching, stamping and weaving linen, which employed 300 hands; mills connected with the woollen trade for 'tucking . . . glossing, smoothing and laying the grain'; a mill for 'knapping' and a leather mill for dressing buckskin; even a paper mill. 'He has been able to erect this multiplicity of mills, thirteen in all, by an uncommon command of water.' (It is interesting that the Mahony family, who bought the woollen mills in 1824, should have provided money to build the village's first Catholic church seventy years later.) Young was a serious agronomist and concerned with agrarian and industrial affairs. Though he describes the Blarney demesne:

> Mr Jeffreys has much improved Blarney castle and its environs: he has formed an extensive ornamented ground, which is laid out with considerable taste; an extensive plantation surrounds a large piece of water and walks lead through the whole. There are several pretty sequestered spots where covered benches are placed . . .

he makes no mention of the famous stone.

The poet and playwright Padraic Colum (1881–1972) in his book *Cross Roads in Ireland*

(1930) retells a legend of the castle that was told him by a fixture at the castle gate: 'Near the gate, under the trees, with a shawl over her head for shelter from the showers, is a simple-faced old woman . . . ' The story she told him 'had to do with water and a fairy woman':

The King of Munster saved an old woman who was about to drown in the lake. She had nothing to give him by way of reward. She told him, however, that if he would mount the topmost wall of his castle, and kiss a stone which she described to him, he would gain a speech that would win friend or foe to him, man or woman.

Might this have been the story that caused the Blarney poet Father Prout to embellish Milliken's poem with the detail of the marvellous stone? There was only one stone that stood out from the rest: the one that Cormac Láidir had set in the wall and that held the details of the date and the founder. The only trouble was that it was very hard to get at.

4

ROMANCING THE STONE

The stone which Cormac Láidir had his masons set was placed high on the face of the tower and if, as romance and local lore insisted, this was the stone that gave the gift of Munster gab, it required considerable courage and dexterity to reach it. By the time Anna and Samuel Hall made their visit the practice of kissing a Blarney stone was well established, and the local parish priest, Reverend Matthew Horgan, whose scholarship they greatly respected, informed them that 'the curious traveller will look in vain for the *real stone*, unless he allows himself to be lowered from the northern angle of the lofty castle when he will discover it about twenty feet from the top . . . ' The difficulty was exacerbated by an event which occurred, as always in these cases, 'a few days before our visit':

. . . a madman made his way to the top of the castle and after dancing round it for some hours, his escape from death being almost miraculous, he flung the stone from the tower; it was broken in the fall and now, as the guide stated to us, the 'three halves' must receive three distinct kisses to be in any degree effective.

Guides have since time immemorial known that their role is as much that of entertainer as of local expert!

Kissing the original Blarney stone was clearly not worth the risk that its position entailed, except for the very foolhardy. Eloquence could be bought at too high a price. The visitor who called himself 'An Oxonian' when he wrote the light-hearted *A Little Tour of Ireland*, makes it clear how hair-raising the early kissing must have been. He begins by commending the view from the tower (which many say is the real thrill of Blarney):

The landscape rewards your exertions, when you have ascended the narrow staircase of the sole remaining tower, and this somewhat resembles ('magna componere') an excellent 'Stilton' which has gone the way of all good cheeses, and is now a hollow ruin – a ruin on which a sentimental mouse might sit, like Marius at Carthage, and bitterly recall the past.

Looking down this cavity, made gloomier by the dark ivy and wild myrtle, which grow from floor to battlements, one feels that fainty thrill and chilliness which is equally unpleasant and indescribable . . .

It was just possible in that position to see the original stone with the Latin inscription:

This is said to be the *original* Blarney Stone, but no man could possibly kiss it, unless . . . he happened to be a bird, or an acrobat, twelve feet long, and suspending himself by his feet from the summit of the tower.

Now it is my conviction, primarily suggested by my own sensations, and subsequently confirmed by what I noticed in others, that the majority of those who kiss the *Blarney Stone* do wish and try to believe in it. We English have so scanty a stock of superstitions, and some of these are so wanting in refinement and dignity . . .

Dr Sean Pettit, the author of the official guide, *Blarney Castle, The Story of a Legend* (1989), records a visit made by Charles Etienne Cosque-bert de Montbret, who was French Consul in Dublin. The year of his tour was 1789, a convenient time to be away from Paris: bliss was it that dawn to be alive, but to be safely in Dublin was very heaven! His itinerary naturally included Cork and he referred to 'Blarney castle on the top of which is a large stone that visitors who climb up are made to kiss, with a promise that in so doing they will gain the privilege of telling lies for seven years.' The guide on duty that day must have had an overdose of the kissing stone himself! By then the stone that the builders had fixed had been dismissed, and the piece of masonry that the growing numbers of

visitors kissed was only a few inches from the top of the tower. The Halls in their provident nineteenth-century and, it must be said, unIrish way, expressed their strong approval that the whiff of danger had departed from the act of kissing:

> The attempt to do so was, indeed, so dangerous, that a few years ago Mr Jeffreys had it removed from the wall and placed on the highest point of the building; where the visitor may now greet it with little risk. It is about two feet square, and contains the date 1703, with a portion of the arms of the Jeffreys family, but the date, at once, negatives its claim to be considered the true marvel.

Even after the relocation of the stone at the top of the tower and the fixing of iron bars to allow the kisser to bend back the head into the necessary position, the occasional visitor found it still too perilous. An example of this may be found in another nineteenth-century book called *A Walking Tour round Ireland in 1865* (1867). Its author, with true Victorian reticence, called himself merely 'An Englishman'. It is clear that by the time of his visit the stone was the main attraction and that the groves which had earlier been the draw had become less popular.

He fell in with his companions as they left the railway station, and found that 'they were all Irish people'. One of them had just come home from India having won the Victoria Cross; he accompanied 'a husband and wife and another lady' and they were joined by a 'Donegal man'.

The Blarney influence seemed to operate immediately on ['the Victoria-Cross man']. He shook me warmly by the hand, and expressed the great pleasure it gave him to make my acquaintance . . .

We sought out the cicerone, who was an old woman with some wit. She took us first into an outhouse and pointed to a small stone very much like an anvil and said, 'There's the Blarney stone.' To this statement we demurred, as absurd, though the husband kissed the stone. No one followed his example. The old woman then said that the real Blarney stone was at the top of the castle, pointing to a large block sustained by iron girders. We therefore ascended the tower. All the party, except the Victoria-Cross man and myself, preceded us, who loitered behind talking. When we reached the summit, the indefatigable husband said that he had just kissed the stone, but recommended that no one else make the attempt. The stone is certainly placed in a dangerous position for the operation of kissing. It is suspended from one side of the tower, with a vacant yawning interval between it and the parapet on which you stand. My friend, who had apparently set his heart on kissing the stone, being probably a bachelor, solemnly took off his hat, approached the place and knelt down, but he quickly returned again, and said he would not make the attempt, as he was not given to do foolish things. His party was amused but none dared to question his courage.

We then descended the tower of the castle, when the party at once announced their intention of proceeding to the village inn to an entertainment they had ordered there, and which evidently formed the most material part of the day's excursion. My friend gave me an invitation to join them there, but I excused myself. The Donegal man and myself, however, persuaded them to come and see the caves, which are curious in their way. Then there was the lake to be seen, but here the resolution of the party fairly gave way. There was the entertainment, from which they could not keep away any longer. So we separated, my friend and I, after such a cordial greeting, parting with a ceremonial bow. The Donegal man and myself now remained, and we started in the direction of the lake, and by the aid of a man who refused to regard himself as a guide, but on our leaving, nevertheless claimed and received a gratuity, we found the sheet of water, and then returned to the entrance of the celebrated Groves of Blarney, so renowned in song. The keeper said he asked the remainder of our party to enter, but they excused themselves on the ground of the entertainment at the inn. We entered the groves, which, though small in extent, are certainly well worth seeing. They consist of a garden, walks and grottos. The custodian, a lame man, is a most conscientious fellow, for, though there is no residence here, and any of the family of the proprietor come to the groves but rarely, yet, unassisted, this man keeps them in the most prim and excellent order, as if a master constantly surveyed his proceedings. Such faithful service, where there is no eye to see nor master to please deserves to be recorded . . .

I was well pleased with my visit to Blarney. True, I had not kissed the stone. I had no wish to do so originally, and the desire did not come with the difficulty; and had the wish been present, I should have deemed it presumptuous to gratify it after the failure of a holder of the Victoria Cross. And looking back at the matter retrospectively, I feel glad not to have kissed the stone, because the reader will now the more readily believe that I am giving a plain truthful account of my travels in Ireland, unaccompanied by any blarney.

5

THE BLARNEY STONE
AND THE DIASPORA

Blarney with its groves, purling streams and stone has remained a beauty spot holding its own with Killarney and beating even the Cliffs of Moher as an absolute requirement for the visitor to Munster or, indeed, to Ireland. Its fame spread overseas, travelling with the many emigrants who left during and after the Great Famine. Many of these were Gaelic speakers since the Famine afflicted especially the areas where Irish was still the first language, the part of Ireland as described by Thomas Davis, the founder of the Young Ireland movement, as west of a north–south line from Derry to Waterford. The English they used in their new homes did not sound much like that spoken by the older emigrants. It was different: softer, unthreatening;

it made use of non–English expressions, and unless the 'Grecian', as the Irish immigrant worker was sometimes called, was drunk or irate, it could be attractive. It certainly sounded delightful in the mouth of a pretty Irish colleen and was soon realised as 'blarney'.

The word, as songwriters soon discovered, rhymed with Barney, a common Irish forename (and one which in lowercase like paddy and indeed Irish, had noisy connotations), and also with Killarney. This gave rise to some Tin-Pan-Alley geographical confusion as in the song 'Did Your Mother Come from Ireland?' which has the line:

'And before she left Killarney, Did your mother kiss the Blarney?'

The lyric writers neither knew nor cared that the distance from Blarney to Killarney, even for a crow, is not less than forty miles. Even more surrealist is the Australian song, 'If We Only had Old Ireland over Here!' which has the line,

'If the Blarney stone stood out in Sydney Harbour'

One song takes the William MacGonagall Prize for easily answered song-title questions: 'Can Anybody Tell me Where the Blarney Roses Grow?'

The nineteenth-century Irish immigrants in Britain, America and Australia took some time to gain respectability. It was the transportable parts of their culture that helped change the public perception of them as lawless, brawling, sluttish and drunken – and in New South Wales as literally ticket-of-leave people. The most portable cultural elements, and ones that prevailed among a people rendered peasants by proscription, were poetry, music and dance. Much 'mountain' music, the Country and Western that intermittently recovers great popularity, has Irish roots, as has barn dancing and line dancing. American Civil War songs such as 'The Bonny Blue Flag' and 'When Johnnie Comes Marching Home' were adapted from Irish originals, the latter hygienised from the black eighteenth-century ballad of a returning soldier, 'Johnny, I Hardly Knew You' with the stark couplet,

> You're an eyeless, noseless, chickenless
>   egg
> You'll have to be put with a bowl to beg.

The immigrant Irish were largely Catholic and, though originally mainly rural, took to ghetto living until they felt free to enter the larger community. As long as they remained a defensive underclass they used an unthreatening and if necessary wheedling – and mystifying – style of chat. Their political rise involved oratorical persuasion which they seemed to have by nature (and this was not confined to natives of Munster, though few sounded as mellifluous). The many bright Irish colleens, as they were relentlessly called, who as nursemaids and tweenies had a remarkable, not to say subversive effect in the grand houses in which they were employed; they sounded a lot better, and were certainly abler at handling English than other immigrant groups.

The Irish the world over, if not at home where there were too many rivals, gained a deserved reputation for effective forensic ability – and blarney. It became the mark of the nineteenth- and earlier twentieth-century stage-Irish, especially in vaudeville and music hall, which meant that when the Talkies, which used a lot of theatrical material, became the great medium of popular entertainment, the reputation of the Irish for fightin' and palaver became permanently established – written in (Blarney) stone, you could say.

Modern nationals with folk memory of blarneying ancestors decided that if maybe they went back someday to Ireland, even at the closing of their days, they would make certain to visit the place where such persuasive power of words was freely available. The source of all that blather was a swift journey across a jet-covered ocean. The Irish in America, Australia and even Britain became conscious of their own reputation for forensic pleading and successful amorous verbal wooing, falling into a blarney-ish mode as it suited their purposes. Their memories of grandparents with 'real brogues' and the inevitable journey to the 'old country' had to include a visit to Blarney.

Today the coach park in Blarney rarely stands empty and the queues on the castle stairs grow ever denser. The mood of the visitors is mellow, soothed by the beauty of the place and the soft southern air. The place is peaceful, without the sense of doom or old unexorcised sorrows that weigh heavily on less blessed parts of the green isle. That special feeling, a surge of blarney, was most exuberantly expressed by a returning exile, John Locke (1817–89) in his poem 'Dawn on the Irish Coast':

> I feel the breath of the Munster breeze,
> Thank God that my exile's ended!
> Old scenes, old songs, old friends again,
> The vale and cot I was born in –
> O, Ireland, up from my heart of hearts,
> I bid you the top of the mornin'!

It is the purest of blarney that all well-disposed visitors to Ireland, however remote their Hibernian claims should feel like exiles returning.

6

ODES TO BLARNEY

Though the Blarney Stone, or more precisely the eloquence that it supplied, featured in songs, recitations and play and film dialogue, it did not inspire the highest poetry. Tennyson took one look at Killarney and wrote, 'The Splendour Falls' which has the true poet's line: 'The long light shakes along the lakes'; the monastic island in the Shannon inspired T. W. Rolleston (1857–1920) to compose a beautiful version of a Gaelic poem as 'The Dead at Clonmacnoise':

> In a quiet water'd land, a land of roses,
> Stands Kieran's city fair;
> And the warriors of Erin in their famous
>   generations
> Slumber there.

and Cashel of Munster generated one of the most touching of all Irish love poems *Caiseal Mumhan*:

> *Phósfainn thú gan bha gan phunt gan áireamh spré*
> *agus phógfainn thú maidin drúchta le bánú an lae.*
> *'S é mo ghalar dúch gan mé is tú, a dhianghrá mo chléibh,*
> *i gCaiseal Mumhan is gan de leaba fúinn ach clár og déil.*

> (I'd wed you without cattle, without money, without dowry itself.
> And I'd kiss you of a dewy morning at daybreak.
> It is my sickness sore that we are not together in Cashel, O love of my heart,
> With only a plank of plain bog-deal for our bed.)

Its only true laureate was 'Honest Dick' Milliken and it is appropriate to give his tributary squib

in full; but first it is only fair also to give the
text of the poem that inspired his effort,
'Castlehyde':

As I roved out on a summer's morning
    down by the banks of the Blackwater
    side,
To view the groves and meadows charm-
    ing, the pleasant gardens of Castle-
    hyde;
'Tis there I heard the thrushes warbling,
    the dove and partridge I now describe;
The lambkins sporting on ev'ry morning,
    all to adorn sweet Castlehyde.

The richest groves throughout this nation
    and fine plantations you will see there;
The rose, the tulip, the sweet carnation,
    all vying with the lily fair.
The buck, the doe, the fox, the eagle,
    they skip and play by the river side;
The trout and salmon are always sporting
    in the clear streams of Castlehyde.

There are fine walks in these pleasant
    gardens, and seats most charming in
    shady bowers.
There gladiaathors both bold and darling
    each night and morning do watch the
    flowers.
There's a church for service in this fine
    arbour where nobles often in coaches
    ride
To view the groves and meadows
    charming, the pleasant gardens of
    Castlehyde.

There are fine horses and stall-fed oxes,
    and dens for foxes to play and hide;
Fine mares for breeding and foreign sheep
    there with snowy fleeces in Castlehyde.
The grand improvements they would
    amuse you, the trees are drooping
    with fruit all kind;
The bees perfuming the fields with music,
    which yields more beauty to Castle-
    hyde.

If noble princes from foreign nations
    should chance to sail to this Irish
    shore,
'Tis in this valley they would be feasted
    as often heroes have been before.
The wholesome air of this habitation
    would recreate your heart with pride;
There is no valley throughout this nation
    in beauty equal to Castlehyde.

I road from Blarney to Castle Barnet, to
    Thomastown, and sweet Doneraile,
To Kilshannick that joins Rathcormack,
    besides Killarney and Abbeyfeale;
The flowing Nore and the rapid Boyne,
    the river Shannon and pleasant Clyde;
In all my ranging and serenading I met
    no equal to Castlehyde.

The nice mixture of pedantry and imprecision
marks the poet as the product – or more likely
the master – of a hedge-school. (And it indicates
that Blarney was known as a demesne of
comparable charm and beauty.) The apparent
pretentiousness was more than Milliken could

resist, especially since his riposte was the result of a challenge on hearing the broadsheet ballad sung at a party, and probably in a broad Cork accent. Milliken was a man of charm and known kindness and honesty but he was true-blue unionist and a member of the Cork yeomanry that had so cruelly suppressed the 1798 rising in Wexford. He had neither empathy with the Gaelic forms and modes that 'Castlehyde' tried to render in English nor sympathy with the people who, penalised from formal education, wanted learning so much that they accepted what they could from the oddly qualified and classically inclined 'academicians'.

Yet we should not take his satire too seriously; it was written in merry mood and largely extempore. And it shows an acquaintance with his subject closer than the unknown rhymster's with Castle Hyde.

The groves of Blarney
They look so charming
Down by the purling
Of sweet silent brooks,
Being banked with posies
That spontaneous grow there,
Planted in order
By the sweet 'Rock Close'.
'Tis there the daisy
And the sweet carnation,
The blooming pink
And the rose so fair,
The daffydowndilly,
Likewise the lily,
All flowers that scent
The sweet, fragrant air.

'Tis Lady Jeffers
That owns this station;
Like Alexander,
Or Queen Helen fair;
There's no commander
In all the nation,
For emulation,
Can with her compare.

Such walls surround her,
That no nine-pounder
Could dare to plunder
Her place of strength;
But Oliver Cromwell,
Her he did pommel
And made a breach
in her battlement.

There's gravel walks there
For speculation
And conversation
In sweet solitude.
'Tis there the lover
May hear the dove, or
The gentle plover
In the afternoon;
And if a lady
Would be so engaging
As to walk alone in
Those shady bowers,
'Tis there the courtier
He may transport her
Into some fort, or
All underground.

For 'tis there's a cave where
No daylight enters,
But cats and badgers
Are for ever bred;
Being mossed by nature,
That makes it sweeter
Than a coach-and-six or
A feather bed.
'Tis there the lake is,
Well stored with perches,
And comely eels in
The verdant mud;
Besides the leeches,
And groves of beeches,
Standing in order
For to guard the flood.

There's statues gracing
This noble place in –
All heathen gods
And nymphs so fair;
Bold Neptune, Plutarch,
And Nicodemus,
All standing naked
In the open air!

So now to finish
This brave narration
Which my poor genii
Could not entwine;
But were I Homer,
Or Nebuchadnezzar,
'Tis in every feature
I would make it shine.

It is likely that it was the poem's regency indelicacy rather than it mocking stage Irishry that really upset Anna Hall.

It was written in 1798 six years before Fr Prout was born so the earliest likely date of his extra verse that had such an effect on Blarney's history would be about 1825. He was a prodigious scholar and entertained himself by making rather free versions of his addition in Latin, Italian and French:

THE BLARNEY STONE

Blarneum Nemus

Fortunam autem
Premuerunt oscula cautem
(Fingere dum conor
Debitus huic sic honor):
Quam bene tu fingis
Qui saxi oracula lingis,
Eliquioque sapis
Quod dedit ille lapis!

Gratus homo bellis
Fit unctis melle labellis,
Gratus erit populo
Oscula dant scopulo;
Fit subito orator,
Caudaque sequente senator.
Scandere vis aethram?
Hanc venerare petram.

THE BLARNEY STONE

Le Bois de Blarnaye

Une pierre s'y rencontre
Estimable trésor.
Qui vaut son poids en or
Au guide qui la montre
Qui baise ce monument
Acquiert la parole
Qui doucement cajole;
Il devient éloquent.

Au boudoir d'une dame
Il sera bien reçu,
Et même a son inscu
Fera naître une flamme.
Homme à bonnes fortunes,
A lui on peut se fier
Pour mystifier
La Chambres des Communes.

THE BLARNEY STONE

I Boschi di Blarnea

Sarò ben basso
Se oltre passo
Un certo sasso
D'alto valor;
In su la faccia
Di chi lo baccia
Perenne traccia
Riman talor:
Quel si distingue
Con usar linge
Pien di lusinghe
Per ingannar:
Famosa Pietra!
Mia umil' cetra
O qui dipongo
Su quest' altar'.

The Blarney Annual (1949–50) which published these jokey versions commissioned the Gaelic scholar Tadhg Ó Donnchadha (1874–1949), who as 'Torna' was one of the leading lights of the Gaelic League, to render the verse into Irish.

Tá cloch le comhacht ann, 's an té do
  phógainn í
Is líofa a ghlórtha in gach aon ócáid;
Le cainnt a bheóil ghlic 'sé mheallfadh
  óigbhean,
Nó dul gan stró ar bith 'na bhall don Dáil.
Is togha cainnteóra do dhéanfaidh fós de,
Nó aighneasóir nach ceart 'dul 'na pháirt';
A bhac ní dóigh dhuit, ná súil le sceón ann,
An cloch ó phóg sé 'sa Bhlárnain.

An alternative, less romantic, view is to be found in an anonymous poem published in *Gems of the Cork Poets*, an anthology edited by Daniel Casey and published in Cork. It is undated but has the slightly rackety air of material published there before the Great Famine blighted everything. The only editorial information given is that it 'appeared in the "Cork Reporter" some years since'. It is called 'Oh Blarney Castle, My Darling' and explains quite a bit about the course of Irish history.

THE BLARNEY STONE

Oh! Blarney Castle, my darling, you're
    nothing at all but a stone,
With a small little taste of ould ivy, that
    upon your side has grown;
Och! it's you that was once strong and
    ancient, and you kept all the Sas-
    senachs down,
And you sheltered the Lord of Clancarty,
    who lived then in Dublin town.

Bad cess to that robber, ould Cromwell,
    and to all his long battering train,
Who rowl'd over here like a porpoise, in
    two or three hookers, from Spain;
And the fellow that married his daughter,
    with a big grape shot in his jaw,
'Twas the bould I-er-ton they called him,
    and he was his brother-in-law.

So they fired off the bullet like thunder,
    and it flew through the air like a
    snake,
And they hit the high walls of the Castle
    which like a young curlew did shake,
While the Irish had nothing to fire but
    their bows and their arrows – 'the
    sowls',
Poor tools for shooting the Sassenachs,
    tho' mighty good for wild fowls.

Now one of the boys of the Castle he
    took up a Sassenach's shot,
And he covered it up with turf ashes, and
    he watched it till it was red hot,
Ten he carried it up in his fingers, and
    he threw it right over the wall,
He'd have burnt their tents all to tinder
    if on them it happened to fall.

The ould Castle it trimbled all over, as
    you'd see a horse do in July
When just near the tail, in his crupper,
    he's teas'd by a pesterin' fly;
Black Cromwell he made a dark signal –
    for in the black art he was deep –
So, tho' the eyes of the people stood
    open, they found themselves all fast
    asleep.

With his jack-boots he stepped on the
    water, and he march'd right over the
    lake,
And his soldiers they all followed after as
    dry as a duck or a drake;
And he gave Squire Jeffreys the castle,
    and the loch, and the rock-close they
    say,
Who both died there, and lived there in
    quiet, as his ancestors do to this day.

(The ghost of Sir Boyle Roche was clearly still
prowling about; it was he who explained that
when he talked about 'posterity' he did not

68

mean 'our ancestors but those who came immediately after them'.)

It is odd and probably significant that Tom Moore who urged Sir Walter Scott to pay his visit in the first place makes no mention of Blarney in his *Irish Melodies*. That other celebrator of the lighter side of Irish life, Dion Boucicault (1820–90) did not set a single one of his 150 plays in Blarney, though it was his transferring of the story of the Colleen Bawn to Killarney from Co Limerick that imposed the 'Colleen Bawn Rock' and 'Danny Mann's Cottage' on Muckross Park and did more for 'Heaven's reflex' than Benedict, Balfe, Falconer and Queen Victoria put together. Even in the three Irish plays which keep his name alive: *The Colleen Bawn* (1860), *Arrah-na-Pogue* (1864) and *The Shaughraun* (1874) I can find no mention of the stone nor its endowments.

No mini-Blarney anthology would be complete without mention of a poem by Torna called 'Caisleán na Blárnann' and published in *The Blarney Annual* of 1948. The third verse mentions the stone:

THE BLARNEY STONE

An seana-nós thug glóir dhon áit
A chomhall ní fuláir gan cháimh gan
  cheataighe:
Cloch 'na choróin 'sa pógadh ar sáinn
Is congnamh d'fhagháil, má's gádh san,
  achtuighim.
Chuir Cormac Mór is Crónán cáidh
De chomhacht san áirdlic tráth dár ghrean í,
Pé duine phógann gheobhaidh dá bhárr
Buadhanna oráide is dáin is ealadhan.

This may be rendered in inappropriate doggerel as:

An antique practice gives the place its
  great fame.
The rules must be followed precisely:
A stone at its apex you kiss without
  shame
But from this deal you do quite nicely.
Cormac Mór and St Crónán, they gave
  it great grace
When they settled the block in that part.
If you risk neck to kiss it you'll find you're
  an ace
At eloquence, poetry and art.

70

THE BLARNEY STONE

I have not been able to determine which of
Ireland's many St Crónáns is referred to here.
Maybe there was a local one but of the four
best-known St Crónáns, those of Tuamgraney
and Roscrea lived nearest and about equidistant
from the stone. After all, perhaps Milliken and
Mahony should remain as Blarney's only true
laureates. It was they who intentionally or not
first drew the world's attention to the beautiful
place and the miraculous stone. The result is a
happy flow of people of all nationalities that
streams into the elegant Munster village to
enjoy again the pleasure of the groves, the
historical redolence of the keep and the efficacy
of the stone. At the height of the tourist season
which lasts longer than other seasons they
examine the Rock-Close, Witches' Kitchen,
Druids' Circle and Sacrificial Altar but most
enthusiastically of all they climb the spiral
stairway (with lay-bys for the breathless and a
necessary means of letting through down-coming
traffic) to the top of the keep. There they cannot
help relish the beauty of the place and applaud
the wisdom of Cormac Láidir and his forebears.
The actual kissing is done supine with legs held

by attentive guide while the wind whistles up through the apertures in the machicolations and ruffles the hair. The neophyte grabs the handbars and lowers the body to kiss the *lapis lapidum*. And eloquence follows as sure as night day – it must; it's what the journey was made for. Sure would I tell ye a word of a lie!

APPENDIX

QUEEN ELIZABETH'S ROLE IN BRINGING THE
WORD 'BLARNEY' INTO THE ENGLISH LANGUAGE

*The queen was merry; her ladies heard with disbelief
the noise of laughing aloud. The cause of her good
humour was known only to her closest advisers: Sir
George Carew, Lord of Munster, had spent the
night at Chiswick and would present his body and
his report at ten o'clock that morning.*

*Her frown returned as she thought of that
troublesome country to the west. It was the severest
drain on her exchequer but it had cost her more
dearly than riches. Essex, whom she dearly loved,
even though she had boxed his ears — that had been
a very satisfactory sound! — might still be alive but
for his Hibernian foolishness. Even Hugh O'Neill,
who had cost her such pain, had been once a friend,
and more than a friend, of the Virgin Queen. She
laughed aloud, again. Now defeated at Kinsale,
Tyrone skulked in hiding somewhere in his damned
green rainy country. The Irish were defeated. Some*

of their wild chieftains were dead or in exile but most had submitted to the crown imperial. From Antrim to Cork (a nightmarish journey, she had been told, through mountains and bog) all the Irish now were tamed. They held their lands under licence and as earls of her realm. She could afford to rejoice. And to make assurance doubly sure (What a good phrase! She must offer it to Master Will. She was in good frame today!) Milord Carew had drawn up a sound device to quell treasonous Ulster by eviction and plantation.

This was the main purport of his dangerous voyage across the stormy Irish Sea. He would present a scheme for plantation of loyal subjects on Ulster lands brought mainly from the southern territories of her kinsman and heir James VI of Scotland. A shiver ran through her arthritic body. Winding-sheet again! Better think of something more cheerful. Yes, that was it: she remembered that Carew would also be bringing with him the sealed document that would show that Cormac MacCarthy, the Lord of Muskerry and Blarney had finally accepted the terms of what her father had called 'surrender and regrant'. The Irish would forsake their uncivilised clan structure and antique ways of inheritance and tenure, and become peers of a united realm. Mac-

Carthy had been the one wild card in her Munster defences. Yet soon he would become an English earl, Baron of Blarney, and help keep the queen's peace. He had already shown his loyalty to Her Royal Majesty when he marched his soldiers to join Mountjoy's at Kinsale and she had no fears about his final compliance. But of all the Munster chieftains he alone had procrastinated. She knew from dispatches that Carew had sent officers daily to MacCarthy's castle in Cork, only to be greeted by soft words, fulsome promises, lavish hospitality — but no scroll of surrender. Finally Carew was forced to go in person, and it was news of that meeting that she impatiently awaited. It had become a sore point and Carew ran the risk of mockery from some at her court who were not his especial friends. As for herself, she was more amused than angered by all the palaver.

A stir without was followed by a tucket on silver trumpets; the queen's emissary from Ireland had arrived. Carew had wisely brought rich tribute from all over the province of Munster. It was carried before him in bales and caskets which Gloriana viewed with her usual greed. She indicated with heavily beringed fingers that she was graciously pleased to accept them. The Lord of Munster came last of the train carrying a leather scroll case.

'My dear Sir George, we are met in happy time. We are pleased to greet again Our Lord of Munster. The tedious but necessary toil of Irish affairs is clearly well in hand. The scheme of plantation you spoke of . . . ?'

Carew bowed and held up the document case.

'And what of the garrulous fellow of County Cork? What of him?'

Carew coloured, bowed deeply to trifle time, visibly drew breath and stammered, 'Y-your Majesty, when last I visited him he again begged more time. He had to wait, he averred, until his own advisers should make some pronouncment upon old laws – Brechouns, or some such barbaric word . . .' His voice tailed away into a helpless silence.

The face of majesty darkened and the chill was felt at Deptford. A deathly silence filled the chamber. Experienced courtiers grasped their daggers and fixed their eyes on the ground in an attempt not to show the shudders they felt. Carew could scarcely bring himself to lift his head.

Then the queen burst out laughing and continued so loud and long that she was in danger of dislodging

*her wig and bursting open the studs of her low-cut
gown. 'This is all Blarney,' she choked between
snorts. 'What he says he never means!"*

*Blarney! The word was repeated with pleasure
through all the crowded court. Blarney: soft en-
couraging speech, pleasant to the ear, but not
necessarily true. Not by the one half! Carew, now
erect again, pronounced the word with manifest
relief. 'Blarney! All Blarney!'*

*The queen echoed him, 'Blarney. I know what
we should do,' she whispered through her laughter.
'We should give that word to Master Shakespeare!
It is truly made for him.'*

SELECT BIBLIOGRAPHY

'An Englishman'. *A Walking Tour round Ireland in 1865*, 1867.

'An Oxonian'. *A Little Tour of Ireland*, 1859.

Carr, –. *Stranger in Ireland*, 1805.

Casey, D. (ed.). *Gems of the Cork Poets*, n.d.

Colum, P. *Cross Roads in Ireland*, 1930.

Crofton Croker, T. *Researches in the South of Ireland*, 1824.

Hall, A.M. & S.C. *Ireland, its Scenery, Characters, etc.*, 1840.

Lewis, S. *Topographical Dictionary of Ireland*, 1837.

Mahony, F. S. *The Reliques of Father Prout*, 1837.

Pettit, S. *Blarney Castle, The Story of a Legend*, 1989.

Young, A. *A Tour in Ireland*, 1778.

The Blarney Annual, 1948–50.
The Blarney Annual of Fact & Fancy, 1951–4.
The Blarney Magazine, 1954–62.